My first book of Animal Babies

©1989 GRANDREAMS LIMITED

First published 1989. This edition published 1990.

Written and illustrated by Anne & Ken McKie.
Colour origination by Columbia Offset (UK) Limited.

Published by
GRANDREAMS LIMITED
Jadwin House, 205/211 Kentish Town Road, London, NW5 2JU.

Printed in Belgium

ISBN 0 86227 651 9

RB5-6

Everyone loves baby animals.
In this book you will find all
kinds of babies from all around
the world.

If you visit a farm or a pets corner in
the zoo you can often hold the young
animals. Sometimes you can also help to
feed them.

Baby animals in the wild
love to play, but their parents
can be dangerous.
We have to see wild animals
in zoos or on nature films.

Remember, don't take
any baby animal away, its
mother will be close by.

Here are some of the babies that you can see on a farm.

How many chicks do the hen and the cockerel have?

You can make friends with all the baby animals on a farm

Here comes the farmer with some food for the calf.

How many ducklings are going for a swim?

especially these hungry little pigs.

Here is the farmer's wife with a baby donkey
and a very young horse. They are both called foals.

Someone has left the gate open. Can you
count the lambs that have got out?

Two little goats play in the field.
They are called kids.

Three little goslings
going for a walk with
mother goose and
father gander.

When you visit the countryside and walk through the fields and woods, you may spot lots of animals and their babies...if you are quiet.

Foxes

Red Deer

Hedgehogs

Rabbits

Badgers

Baby animals and their parents.

Human family

Reindeer

Porcupines

Leopards

Cattle

Swans

Sheep

Kangaroos

In the zoo some baby animals are easy to handle.

Zebra

Llama

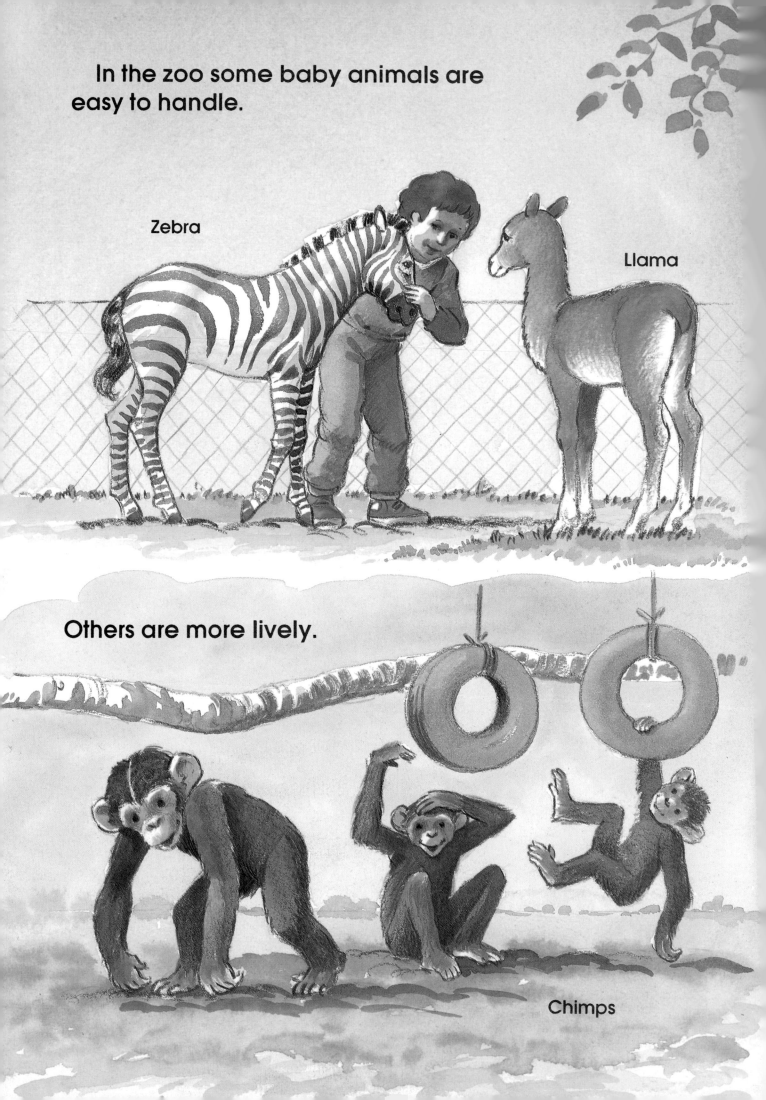

Others are more lively.

Chimps

These baby animals are soft and furry.

Koala

Raccoon

Giant Panda

Some baby animals are very big and heavy.

Giraffe

Elephant

Hippo

Rhino

Other baby animals are very small.

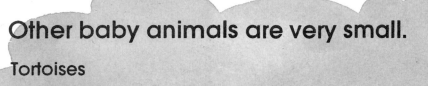

Tortoises

Squirrels

Skunks

Mice

Quail chicks

These baby animals live in very cold countries.

Seals

Polar bears

Penguins

These baby animals live in very hot countries.

Kangaroo

Camel

Lion

Wild pigs

Some baby animals look very soft and cuddly when they are babies, but they grow up to be very dangerous in the wild.

Tiger

Lions

Crocodiles

Wolves

Grizzly bears

Do you have a favourite soft toy shaped like a baby animal?

This little bear likes his Teddy bear.